LIQUID CRYSTAL

C000132625

Poppy Cockburn is a Margate-based writer and communications professional working in the arts. This is her fourth pamphlet of poetry.

Also by Poppy Cockburn

feed notes   (If a Leaf Falls, 2021)

Waiting Room   (Invisible Hand, 2021)

everywhere swans   (Bottlecap Press, 2022)

Liquid Crystal Lovesick Demon

Poppy Cockburn

ISBN: 978-1-915760-95-1

Cover designed by Aaron Kent

Edited by Charlie Baylis

Typeset by Aaron Kent

Broken Sleep Books Ltd
Rhydwen
Talgarreg
Ceredigion
SA44 4HB

Broken Sleep Books Ltd
Fair View
St Georges Road
Cornwall
PL26 7YH

Contents

I'm only an image of what you see.
You don't know me
 — Empress Of, *Woman is a Word*

plot objectives

Do you want it to be about a black orchid bathed in Hitchcockian light, positioned on a sweat-dewed pillow, a killer-lover's note? Or about a Trojan rose with all its thorns concealed inside? Do you want it to be about a man whose skin falls off, who replaces it with poppy petals and no one questions it? Do you want it to be about a broken daisy chain? Or a painting of a waterlily pond that recurs in bad dreams? About a blossom tree that only blooms if you sing to it in the mornings in a soft, low croon? Do you want it to be about a garden that shimmers, makes onlookers feel delirious? And if it isn't, if it's just about the grass that grows and carries on growing, will you accept it? Will you lie in it and try to be happy?

overshare

I admit I'm addicted
to washing salmon fillets
in public squares
then laying them out to dry
in the sun.

Each time, as the
nervous clock ticks by
I wonder whether
they might dry faster
in the privacy of a home,
taste more flavoursome.

Whether I might then
eat them myself

instead of the seagull
whose beaded gaze
follows my reddening face,
my ravenous eyes.

image description

Two tiny moons.
One rippling on the ground.
The other, a wide-open eye
watching unblinkingly from
its starry vantage a third
tiny moon – pale, pressed deep
into a tree's arc, plundered,
flecked in moon milk. Bright
against the bark.

Stella McCartney bra

Iris smiling
Cecile singing
Anna whispering
Fleur humming
Jemima joking
Sylvia laughing
Juliet basking
Phoebe painting
Rose revelling
Caroline reading
Gertrude gyrating
Suzy smirking
Rachel rolling
Cindy seething
Rhiannon ironing
Amelia moaning
Agnes crawling
Gloria writhing
Emily smoking
Ella gargling
Sophie spluttering
Rita menstruating
Celia choking
Kate puking
Shannon shrieking
Olivia bucking
Celeste grinding
Gina gagging
Jasmine watching
Tina floating
Janey sucking
Sinead retching

Mia glaring
Rosie scheming
Lila spitting
Kim sinking
Sandy changing
Eilish blaspheming
Ophelia drowning
Sarah screaming
Cressida hissing
Iris smiling
Cecile singing
Anna whispering

liquid crystal lovesick demon

I slip on a filter,
radiate remote pheromones
and you slide in, follow the protocol:
wyd male order.

I watch the haze-haloed moon
through the misted window,
through the hearts in my eyes.

♥

Your knock on the door
sounds implausibly loud,
your thereness so actual.

I unpause the music —
ambient harp, lamplight
and we're safe again, pretending.

You kiss my synthetic skin,
my plumped-up lips,
caress the budding horns
protruding from my forehead,
apply a finger to my static nosebleed.

♥

I wake once in the night,
horns retracted, head resting
on your patterned torso.

In the morning, I feign sleep,
let you stealth away, keep a picture
of me demonic, cheeks flushed
unnatural rose.

long stretches of no dialogue

Just because we're not talking,
doesn't mean nothing is happening…

Look at my knee.
Look at the sperm-like creatures
squirming towards the moon,
giant moth holes in the blanket
that was meant to keep us numb.

The barking colours. Couples fucking
outdoors in winter, in between hills
the shape of sad eyebrows.

Do you remember when we got
married in a swimming-pool chapel
and I had to swim to the altar
swathed in translucent promises?
All those black petals…

How far can you twist an existence
to avoid the emphatic silence
of slaughter houses?

In certain lights, water looks like blood.

float w me

The afternoon is setting and still
I haven't asked if what happened
means anything to you.

[I don't follow what I want.
I do all I can to thwart]

In a dynamic, who turns the
other onto / off smoking?

[I tell everyone I suck
though I know I don't]

I want to ask you to float w me

but instead
desire-doodled cigarette papers
sink to the bottom of a thought
and saturate, stay there.

sweet creep

Mr Whippy wants my heart

to get me 99 flake fresh

till I swoon beneath the cream
of the sky's lactic tongue.

Let's be kids again —
aren't we having fun?

desire lines, a thread

It's you, it's you, it's all for you, everything I do...

|

Memory: a former love, and me, in bed, in the early morning, asleep. Zoom in. My drowsy lips kissed into the scar on his back. A simple scene turned impossible dream, archived.

|

Passionfruit tastes tart. The tang is satisfying, like pain. I eat one every day.

|

I'm stuck on a thorn, a man. I reach up, tearing at petal edges that return shreds. I recall the apex of his clean-shaven chin digging into my thigh's porcelain then higher, higher. A shattering.

|

He gripped my shoulders as though I was his and said *you make me feel artistic.* He left voicemails describing his new girlfriend.

|

I implore internet strangers to send comforting memes, and they kindly oblige. They send images of birds that look like they've been twice-divorced. I laugh, because they truly do.

|

I notice the neighbour watering his houseplants at night. It comforts me to imagine him asleep alone – a comrade.

|

I have made a playlist of tender moments, one for each lover. I play it on repeat, over and over, a lulling brand of masochism.

|

Ask me anything.

smut observatory

       clouds connect / kiss

their flossy wisps
           moisten / melt
             in The Mouth

    hazy congregation

                sky orgy of easy embraces
                        fluidity

      graceful comings and goings
      cirrus & cumulus – an ONS love story

party atmosphere

         from beneath

          I watch

Blue Velvet

On re-watching, I recall the last time, with an ex.
Back then, I was purely content to have someone
with whom to watch weird films — a rose period of
double-bills and G&T nights in, soaking in pink-on-
pink-on-pink interiors, replacing our thin curtains
with Rothko-red velvet.

Every room has the scope to be a stage. All it takes
is a few choice props to blur the edges — sapphire
eyeshadow, blushed cheeks, high heels the colour
of suburban roses and slow gestures that staccato
like Braques, a woman impatient to be painted pink
is all it takes, to fill the ears with ants, to stop time.

In lamplight, lashes jewelled with tears, Dennis Hopper
appears troublingly beautiful. Seduction depends on
a sensory composition: the lull of an evening's rhythm,
rumbling voices, old-world music, enigmatic glimpses,
souvenir fragrance – a plush spell.

Rookies rarely stand a chance. *In dreams, you're mine
all of the time*. A radiant vacuum halts its expansion
a flower collapses into wisps into nothing [time-lapse].
Is it possible to trust a man, who lugs the figure of a
nude woman in his arms, while professing his love for
another? On reflection, even forgiveness can be warped,
made monstrous.

gorgeous men

cut

crudely
into moist, malleable
icing / take

slice-after-slice

pink
        cream
                softening
                        lips

bid   to   sate
crumb-smeared
craving

hundreds & thousands

[girls girls girls]

honey waves

all-you-can-eat
nostalgia

        stale sugar

nausea

viewing loop

gilded binoculars
are good for
merging entire
shiny worlds
into a single
cycloptic vision
mirrors are obstacles
you can overdose on
men in masks
and metaphysics
double, triple, quadruple
expose yourself
till you are ten-legged
till you are
multi-mouthed
monster
then see if anyone
can kiss you

Comedy

The man was like the Cheshire Cat.

His floating leer

              appeared

                     disappeared

reappeared closer

                 above me

looming down.

             I was very low, on a pavement perhaps
             though I couldn't feel it beneath me, the way
             one often doesn't feel things in dreams.

His stained cat-teeth morphed into a serrated grin.

                *

Then, I magicked my body parts away
vanished

             my throat

my arms

my chest

the cleft between my legs

conjured negative space

in all the places

a man might try a knife.

Only to wake screaming
reassembled.

*

Later, in the mirror
I noticed how the sutures

echoed the shape
of the Cheshire Cat's smile

and smiled.

key words

impulsive

fears

passing

youth

beauty

the end

of everything

sparkly

spent

money

recklessly

husbands

lovers

overdosed

paracetamol

Veuve Clicquot

sparkle

lost

woman

SOURCE: https://www.theguardian.com/uk-news/2015/dec/02/court-grants-impulsive-self-centred-mother-permission-to-die

insights

Today, a lemonade wound will dissolve your principles.
Your mind – become comfortable manufacturing sinkhole realities
– will be swayed by wet blanket temptations that hinder the way
you articulate the angles of your world and lead to millstone sex.

Swap lives with your projections. It won't help to wallow in
action movies or bend yourself out of shape to please a mirror.
Sunsets of opportunity appear in padlocked windows. Start
drawing horizons. Pay attention to their heartbeats.

You are learning true things and feeling committed to creative
safe words, which, it transpires, are the crux of emotional shower
singing.

Stella McCartney bra

Iris smiling
Cecile smiling
Anna smiling
Fleur smiling
Jemima smiling
Sylvia smiling
Juliet smiling
Phoebe smiling
Rose smiling
Caroline smiling
Gertrude smiling
Suzy smiling
Rachel smiling
Cindy smiling
Rhiannon smiling
Amelia smiling
Agnes smiling
Gloria smiling
Emily smiling
Ella smiling
Sophie smiling
Rita smiling
Celia smiling
Kate smiling
Shannon smiling
Olivia smiling
Celeste smiling
Gina smiling
Jasmine smiling
Tina smiling
Janey smiling
Sinead smiling

Mia smiling
Rosie smiling
Lila smiling
Kim smiling
Sandy smiling
Eilish smiling
Ophelia smiling
Sarah smiling
Cressida smiling
Iris smiling
Cecile smiling
Anna smiling

dark horse

wild
a mare
an absolute mare
slick sweat gleaming
nostrils flared steaming
erratic eyes black marbles
impatient flank
hot primitive musk
scuffed hooves proof
of so much longing
to conquer terrain
to own it
with animal body
feel how it makes
the heart race
but first
strap me up
turn me into
a pony girl
I want to be
whipped
by you

To feel something

try voluptuous magpies, leaf fall, neck exposure,
erogenous daydreams, grazings. Backwards walk
through winking streets. Avoid pools of angel tears.

Squint at airplanes caught pink in winter light,
white squirrels crawling up and down electricity
poles, car wheels on wet road [dank soundscape].

Notice interiors: a muted, diner-coloured world,
pearls strung obscenely low, lowering the sun,
plastic trout nailed to matte wall, pastel purity
interrupted by a creeping tentacle.

Sense slick dread oozing, moss muffling ecstasy
o eyes [zoomed in too close].

Listen as saxophone notes curl into the soft night,
as cigarette smoke strokes bodies into yielding states,
wallpapered hearts peeling in red-stained rooms.

slow glimpse

Every time I saw him
I was on bike, he on foot,
staring after me, a blur;
my face, sharp.

He was always holding out
a video tape —
wanted me to stop, take it,
watch it, replay.

I had a similar tape at home
I'd been trying to tape over
but, multiple exposures
rarely turn out.

I only had the one tape
and I fucked it.

excuses excuses

the pink-tinted sea is not calm or reflective
the cat at the window feigns patience
a letter arrives addressed to my neck and I forget to blush
geese gather, menace a response

my laptop warms while I jump between tabs
non-alcoholic alcohol is not what I want
I prefer authentic lemonade
too much male kindness is a swamp [double-cream]

I'm rummaging for excuses not to *tb x*
like digital regulation, like crystals give me anxiety
like I'm looking for a lover with a heart full of art deco swimming pools
who will reel me in, slide the flesh from my bones [slowly]

avoidance is a void is a playscape is better than a drawer full of cutlery
and hey! look over there! the clouds are in a beautiful formation
…if you like, you can keep a pebble from my special pebble collection

meanwhile, I'll float off on a lilo

    and when I'm far enough away

                                I'll start to love you

what I mean to say is, I love you

spat on by the sky for years
praying for a deluge
every day a failed séance
cold communion, unoccupied citadel
nothing deep enough to swim in
switching red lights on and off
trying to ignore the jam jar wasps

only to one day feel the nudge of a new idea
a dawning darkness
to army-crawl into the heart-lit wilderness of yourself
and feel safe there in its boundlessness
its dreamable intimacy

[this account has been deleted]

Notes on the text

'Lovesick Demon' is the name of an Instagram filter. The first line in *desire lines, a thread* is taken from Lana del Rey's song *Video Games*. *Stella McCartney bra* refers to the prominent fashion designer's underwear line, for which each underwear set was formerly titled after a femme name and verb.

Acknowledgements

Thank you to the editors of *SPAM Zine, Footprints: an anthology of new ecopoetry*, and *Perverse*, where versions of these poems have previously appeared. Huge thanks to Charlie Baylis for editorial advice, and to Aaron Kent. Thanks to Chrissy Williams, whose poetry workshop 'Writing after David Lynch' inspired four of the poems in this pamphlet. Thanks also to Caroline Druitt, Karólína Rós Ólafsdóttir, Mau Baiocco, Jack Lenton, Maura Dooley, Ellen McAteer, Jenny Moore and F* Choir. Thanks to K, F, and S.

♥

LAY OUT YOUR UNREST

Ingram Content Group UK Ltd.
Milton Keynes UK
UKHW010803130323
418477UK00005B/925